Special Symbols:

This book is organized to guide the individual through the training. In ad
Notes section there are a number of symbols used to help the participant throughout the presentation and workshop. For your convenience these symbols are repeated at the introduction of each section of this workbook.

Suggestion:

This symbol represents a suggestion or is a general statement relating to facilitation of the training.

Tip:

This symbol represents a tip to the Facilitator and is specific to the concept that the Facilitator is presenting.

Question:

This symbol represents a question that may be asked to the Facilitator or to the participants in the workshop. It is intended to foster interaction during the training.

Table of Contents

Section 1

Section 2

Section 3

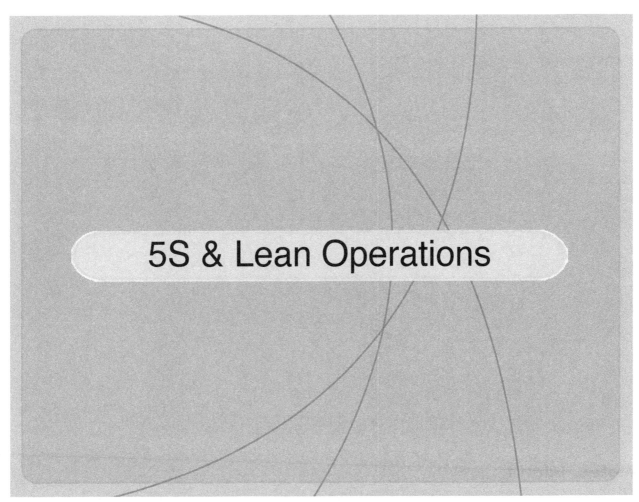

Participant Workbook

In this Section

- Learn the context of 5S
- Discover how 5S fits into improvement projects
- Study the 7 Wastes of Operations

Participant Workbook Provided To:

_____

 Suggestion   **Tip**   **Question**

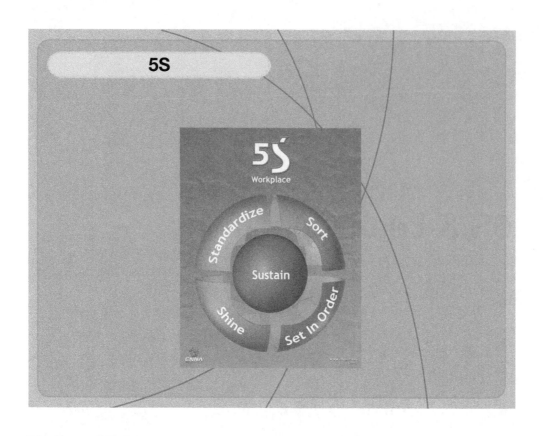

Notes, Slide 1:

_____

_____

_____

_____

_____

_____

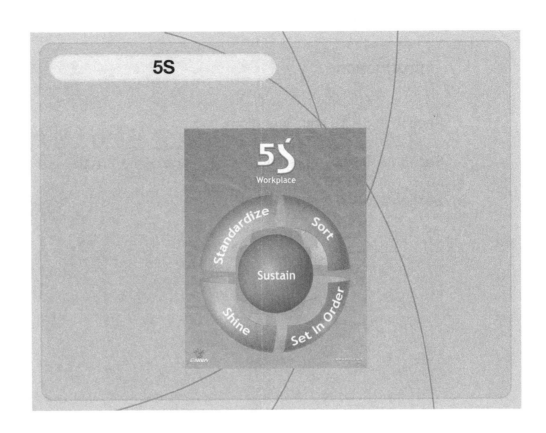

Notes, Slide 1 continued:

_____

_____

_____

_____

_____

_____

_____

Tip:
Pay particular attention to the Facilitator when learning about a clean operation.

Question:
What do people generally think of an operation that is clean?

_____

_____

_____

Introduction

- Section 1: 5S & Lean Operations

- Section 2: 5S & Organization: Each Piece of the Puzzle

- Section 3: 5S & Teamwork

Notes, Slide 2:

_____

_____

_____

_____

_____

_____

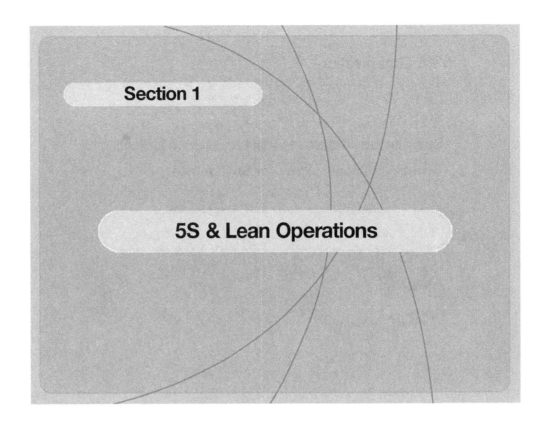

Notes, Slide 3:

_____

_____

_____

_____

_____

_____

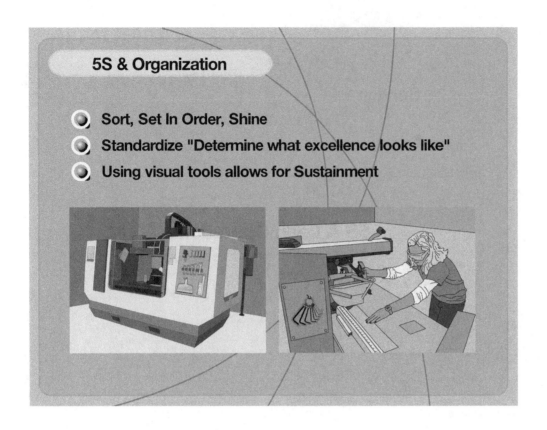

Notes, Slide 4:

_____

_____

_____

_____

_____

_____

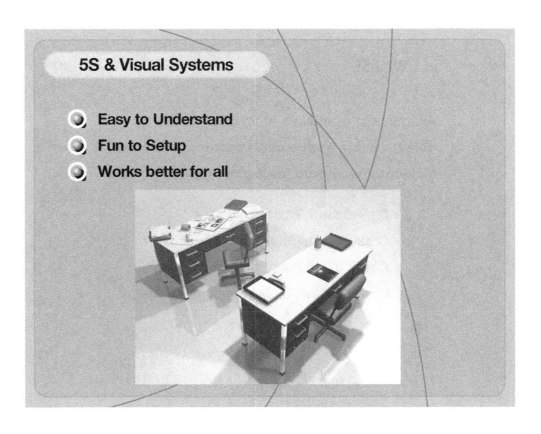

Notes, Slide 5:

_____

_____

_____

_____

_____

_____

Question:

Can you think of any kind of job that may require the need to be visual?

_____

_____

_____

Why 5S

- Allows us to maintain a more organized area
- Able to clean less and clean easier
- Makes our work area more productive

  - Makes the 7 Wastes obvious
  - Creates a standard for improvement
  - A way to get many people involved
  - Low real cost, high-impact for company

Notes, Slide 6:

_____

_____

_____

_____

_____

_____

Question:

Why are we doing 5S?

_____

_____

_____

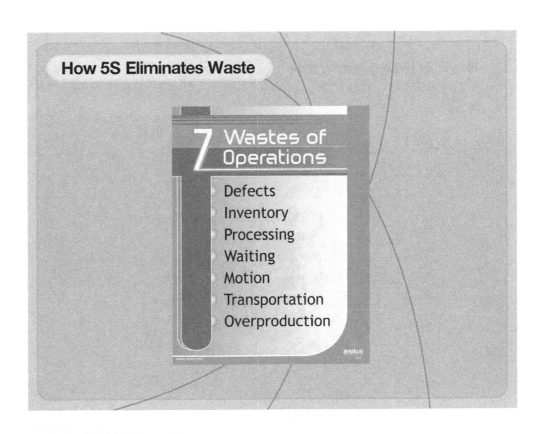

Notes, Slide 7:

Tip:
Focus on the 7 Wastes and what the definitions are.

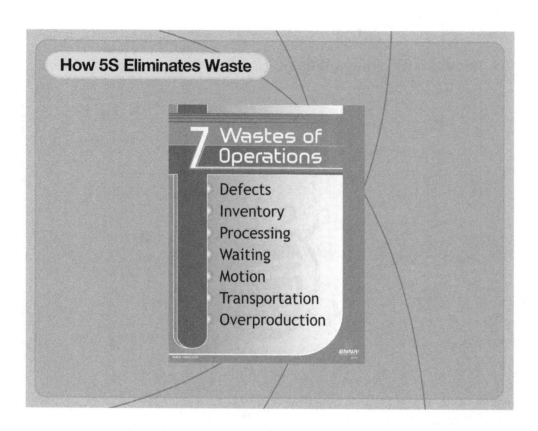

Notes, Slide 7 continued:

_____

_____

_____

_____

_____

_____

Tip:
The 7 Wastes are a fundamental building block of 5S. Ask the facilitator to fully explain the wastes so that you understand them completely.

Defects

Making bad parts, having scrap, wrong information, and/or having to rework items.

Possible Causes:

- Batch Processing
- Quality materials
- Questionable product design
- Poor work instructions

Notes, Slide 8:

_____

_____

_____

_____

Waste Definition: _____

_____

Additional Example: _____

_____

Inventory

Any material in the area other than what is immediately needed for the next process, stage, or step.

Possible Causes:

- Long lead times
- Supplier reliability
- Reward based on output
- Just-in-case logic
- Poor scheduling
- Unknown market demand

Notes, Slide 9:

_____

_____

_____

_____

Waste Definition: _____

_____

Additional Example: _____

_____

Question:

What are the three stages that inventory lives as in your company?

_____

_____

_____

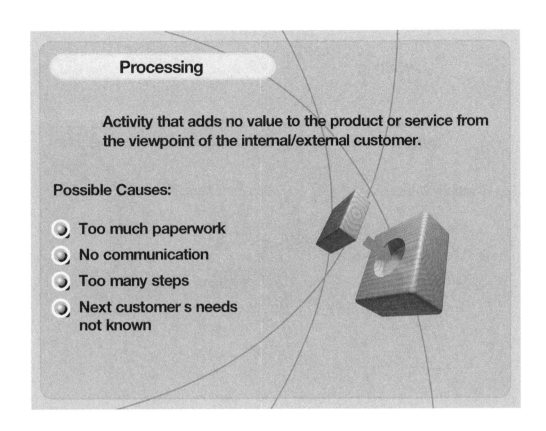

Processing

Activity that adds no value to the product or service from the viewpoint of the internal/external customer.

Possible Causes:

- Too much paperwork
- No communication
- Too many steps
- Next customer s needs not known

Notes, Slide 10:

_____

_____

_____

_____

_____

Tip:
This is the hardest waste to find. However, the solution is simple. If you think about it, if it is truly a waste of over processing, then the ultimate solution is to find a way to not do it.

Waste Definition: _____

_____

Additional Example: _____

_____

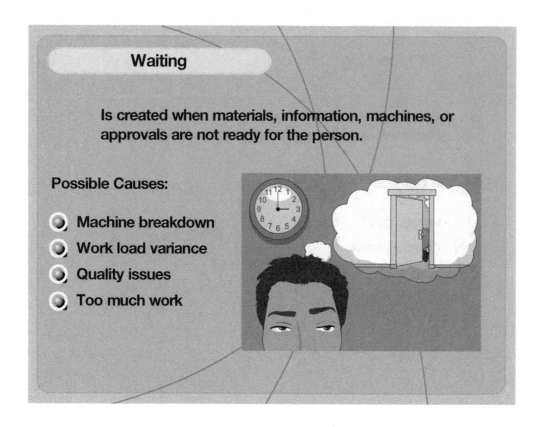

Notes, Slide 11:

_____

_____

_____

_____

Waste Definition: _____

_____

Tip:
Try purposely waiting rather than doing something. It is hard to wait.

Additional Example: _____

_____

Question:

What are some times that you have waited? What are you waiting for?

_____

_____

_____

Motion

Any movement that does not add value to the product or service.

Possible Causes:

- Lack of process design
- No standard work methods
- Design of work area
- Too much in an area

Notes, Slide 12:

_____

_____

_____

_____

Waste Definition: _____

_____

Additional Example: _____

_____

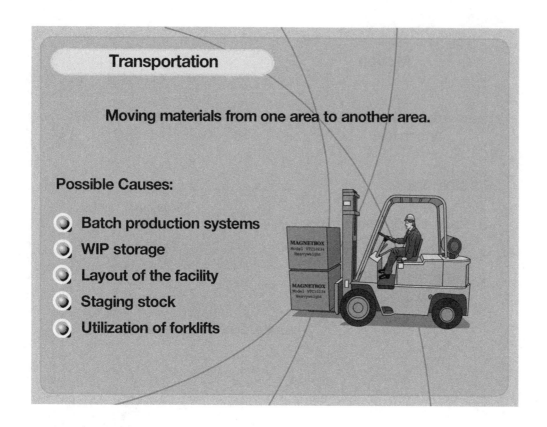

Transportation

Moving materials from one area to another area.

Possible Causes:

- Batch production systems
- WIP storage
- Layout of the facility
- Staging stock
- Utilization of forklifts

Notes, Slide 13:

_____

_____

_____

_____

Waste Definition: _____

_____

Additional Example: _____

_____

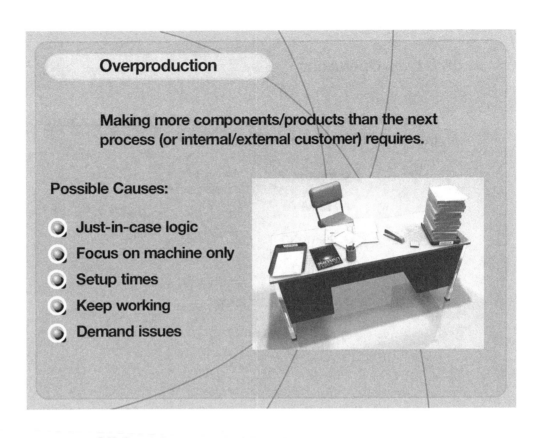

Overproduction

Making more components/products than the next process (or internal/external customer) requires.

Possible Causes:

- Just-in-case logic
- Focus on machine only
- Setup times
- Keep working
- Demand issues

Notes, Slide 14:

Tip:
Operations should look at ways to only produce what is truly needed. Anything more will result in loss of efficiency and effectiveness.

_____

_____

_____

_____

_____

Waste Definition: _____

_____

Additional Example: _____

_____

Question:
Why is overproduction so detrimental to an organization?

_____

_____

_____

5S & Lean Operations

Most, if not all, of the essential tools of Lean have the 5S as the key building blocks.

Examples:

- TPM
- Kanban
- SMED
- Visual Management
- Office Kaizen

Notes, Slide 15:

_____

_____

_____

_____

_____

_____

5S & Organization:
Each Piece of the Puzzle

Participant Workbook

In this Section

- The meaning behind 5S
- Applying 5S in your area and environment
- The five elements of 5S
- Guide for participants through the proper sequence of
  learning 5S

 Suggestion   **Tip**   **Question**

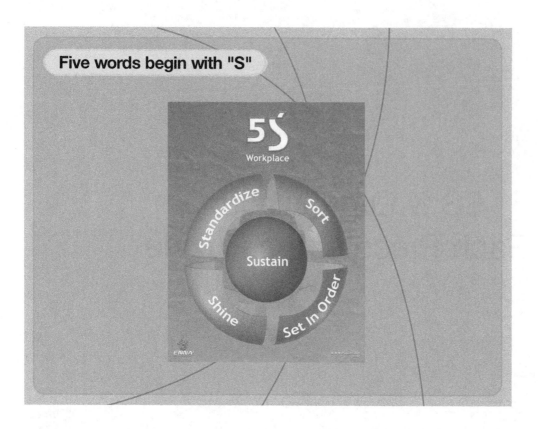

Notes, Slide 17:

_____

_____

_____

_____

_____

_____

Question:

How many S's were there originally and which company founded the term?

_____

_____

_____

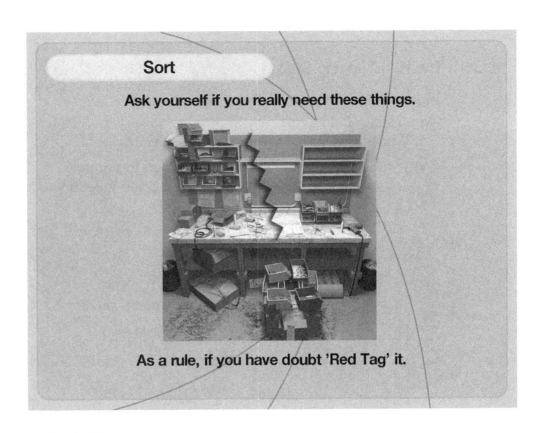

As a rule, if you have doubt 'Red Tag' it.

Notes, Slide 18:

Tip:
When sorting, make two categories:
1) what is needed for the job, and
2) everything else.

_____
_____
_____
_____
_____

Sort Action Defined: _____

_____

Additional Example: _____

_____

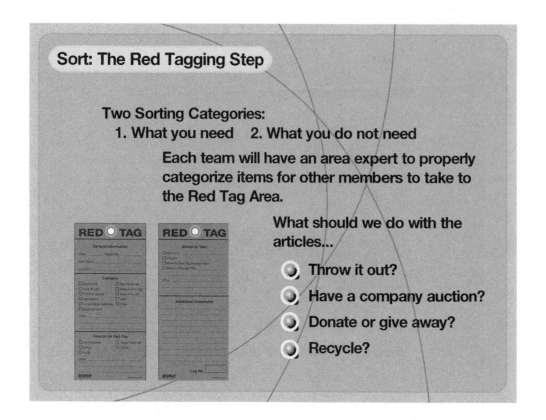

Sort: The Red Tagging Step

Two Sorting Categories:
1. What you need   2. What you do not need

Each team will have an area expert to properly categorize items for other members to take to the Red Tag Area.

What should we do with the articles...

- Throw it out?
- Have a company auction?
- Donate or give away?
- Recycle?

Notes, Slide 19:

_____

_____

_____

_____

_____

_____

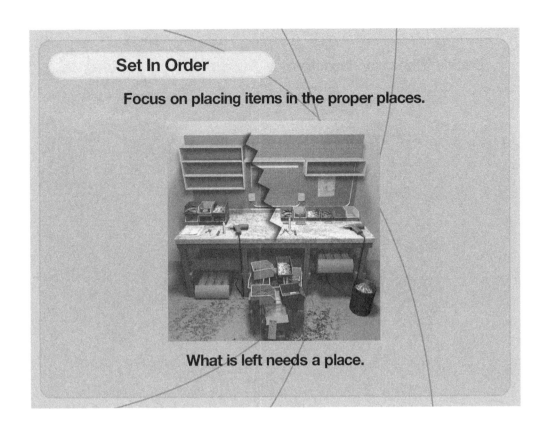

Set In Order

Focus on placing items in the proper places.

What is left needs a place.

Notes, Slide 20:

_____

_____

_____

_____

Set In Order Action Defined: _____

_____

Additional Example: _____

_____

Decide Where to Place Items

Notes, Slide 21:

_____

_____

_____

_____

_____

_____

Tip:
Look at the above illustration. What workstation solutions can you find that minimize the waste of motion?

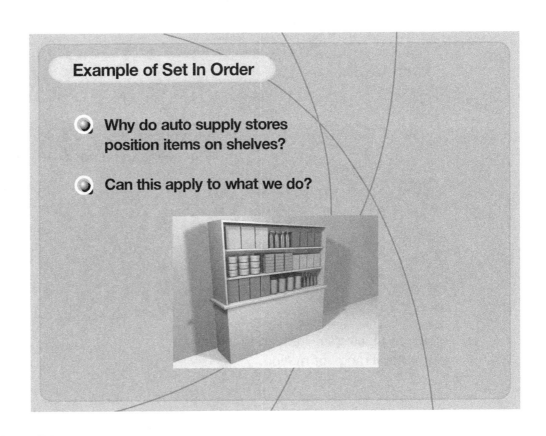

Notes, Slide 22:

_____

_____

_____

_____

_____

_____

_____

Tip:
Try to reach for anything in your work area. The goal of Set In Order is to eliminate reaching.

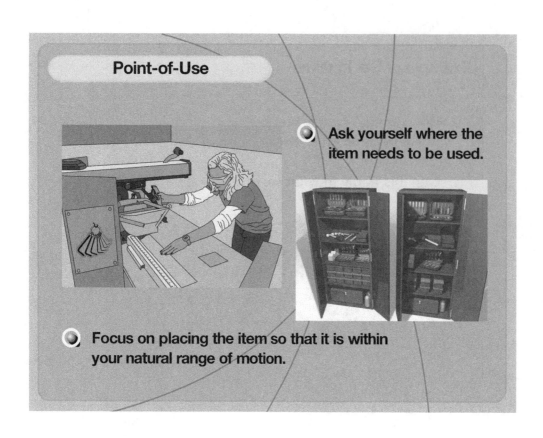

Notes, Slide 23:

_____

_____

_____

_____

_____

_____

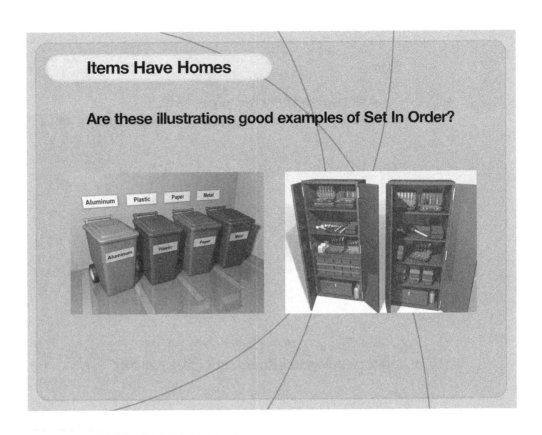

Notes, Slide 24:

Tip:
Use Set In Order to get
working, rather than just
preparing to work.

_____

_____

_____

_____

_____

_____

_____

_____

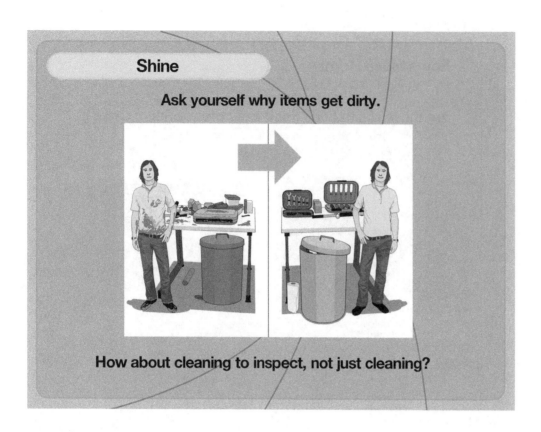

Shine

Ask yourself why items get dirty.

How about cleaning to inspect, not just cleaning?

Notes, Slide 25:

_____

_____

_____

_____

_____

_____

Additional Example: _____

_____

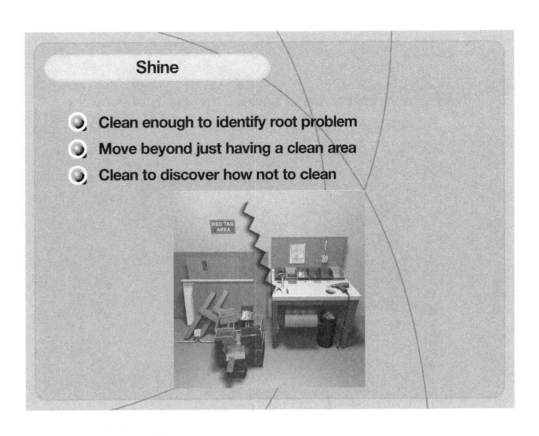

Shine

- Clean enough to identify root problem
- Move beyond just having a clean area
- Clean to discover how not to clean

Notes, Slide 26:

Tip:
Remember, we are cleaning to...

_____

_____

_____

_____

Shine Action Defined: _____

_____

Additional Example: _____

_____

Question:

Why are we cleaning during this workshop?

_____

_____

_____

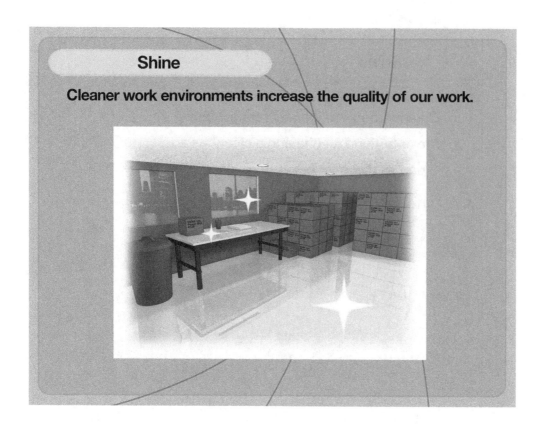

Shine

Cleaner work environments increase the quality of our work.

Notes, Slide 27:

_____

_____

_____

_____

_____

_____

Tip:
Combining ideas together will find solutions to reducing and even eliminating the need for shining.

Standardize

Ask yourself how to create a work area free of checklists.

Once you see it, you know what needs to be done even without years of experience.

Notes, Slide 28:

_____

_____

_____

_____

_____

_____

Question:

Can you think of an example of good standardization?

_____

_____

_____

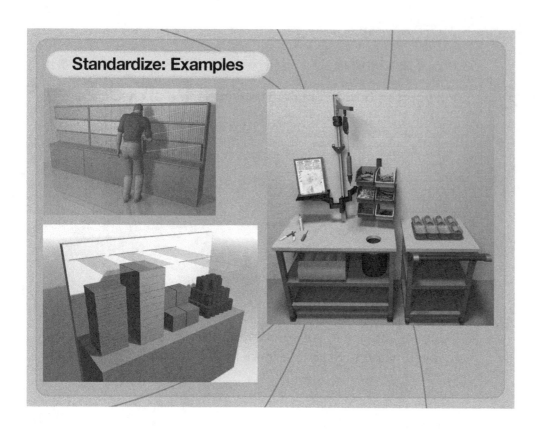

Standardize: Examples

Notes, Slide 29:

_____

_____

_____

_____

Standardize Action Defined: _____

_____

Additional Example: _____

_____

Tip:
When creating a standard, incorporate a symbol, color, and/or physical characteristics.

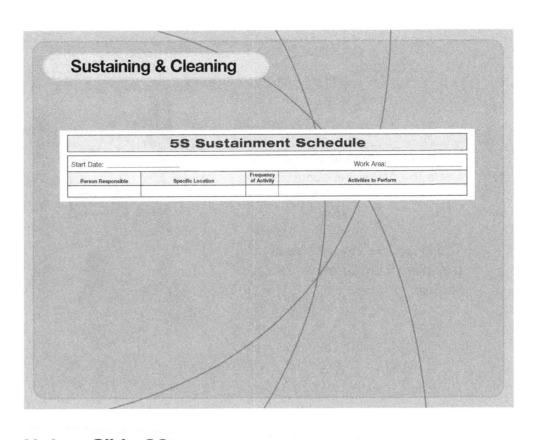

Notes, Slide 30:

_____

_____

_____

_____

_____

_____

Question:

Why is it useful to employ the 5S Sustainment Schedule?

_____

_____

_____

_____

Sustain

Keep asking how to simplify the issue to ensure it is sustained.

The idea: if we have less self-discipline it will be easier to sustain.

Notes, Slide 31:

_____

_____

_____

_____

_____

_____

Question:

What is the ultimate goal of 5S?

_____

_____

_____

Sustain

- Management shows commitment to program
- Everyone leads by being an example of 5S
- 5S is a component of every workshop
- Goal is to have customers tour your facility
- Use the Evaluating 5S Forms to assess 5S score

Notes, Slide 32:

_____

_____

_____

_____

_____

Tip:
Use your past employment experience to help develop sustaining changes. Often past examples help develop solutions. Pull examples from the past and see how the team can use them.

Sustain Action Defined: _____

_____

Additional Example: _____

_____

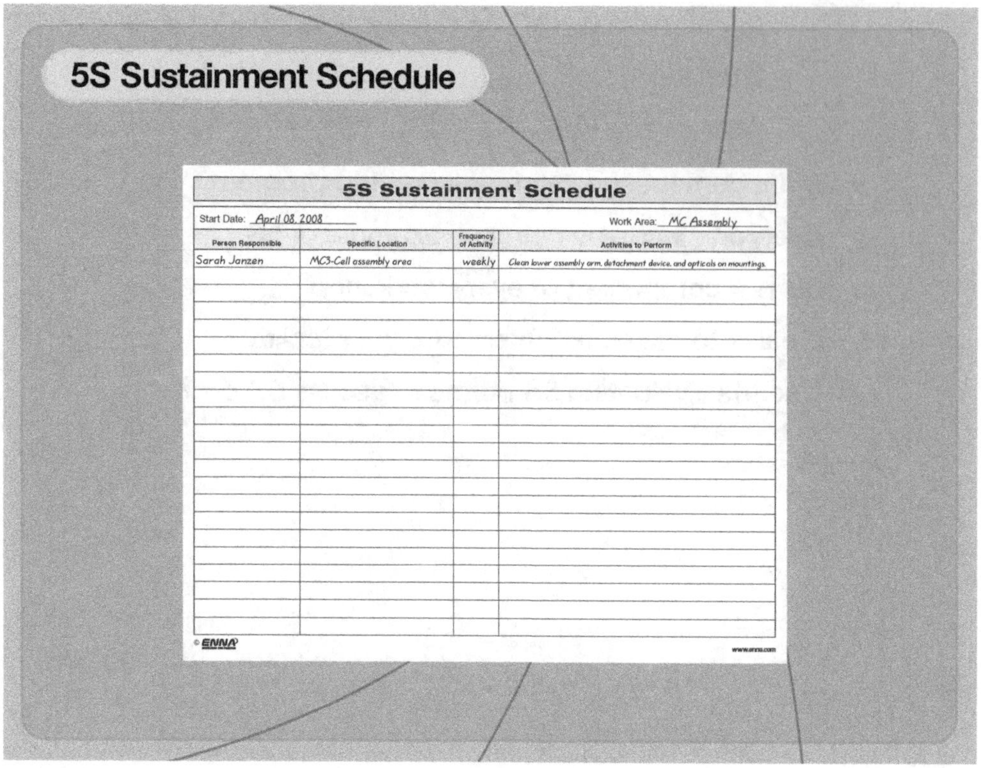

5S Sustainment Schedule

Notes, Slide 33:

_____

_____

_____

_____

_____

_____

Long-Term 5S Success

- Management is expected to be involved in activities
- Involvement of everyone
- 7 Wastes are an integral part of 5S
- Link improvement to a financial benefit

Notes, Slide 34:

_____

_____

_____

_____

_____

_____

Question:

5S needs the commitment of who?

_____

_____

_____

Review & Summary

○ What are the 5S words?

○ Which S is the most important?

○ Can you relate to the need for 5S?

○ What are the 7 Wastes?

○ What is your responsibility?

Notes, Slide 35:

_____

_____

_____

_____

Final thoughts on this section: _____

_____

_____

Tip:
Write down the answers
to these questions to
summarize this section.

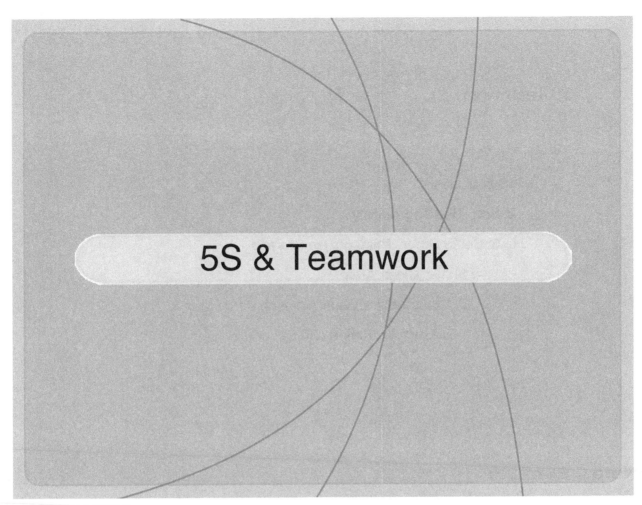

5S & Teamwork

Participant Workbook

In this Section

Now that we have gained some knowledge we are going to put it into practice.

– Learn the 5S evaluation process
– Learn the 30 Day Action Log
– Learn the 5S Sustainment Schedule
– Discuss the workshop format

 Suggestion   **Tip**   **Question**

5S Teamwork

Steps:

1: 5S Evaluation

2: Sort- Red Tag Activity

3: Set In Order- Point of Use Storage

4: Shine- Clean Area

5: Standardize- Visual Management

6: Sustain- Refine and Schedule

Notes, Slide 37:

_____

_____

_____

_____

_____

_____

5S Team

1. Evaluating 5S Team (2-3 people)

2. Photography Team (2 people)
   - Take pictures of the current state
   - Highlight key objects and areas

3. 5S Mapping Team (2-3 people)
   - Layout where people, materials, and equipment should be located (bird s eye view)

Notes, Slide 38:

Tip:
You will change roles as you move from assessment through to making changes, but your team should stay together.

Team Assigned To: _____

Team Members Names: _____

_____

Assigned Work Area:

_____

Additional Information: _____

_____

_____

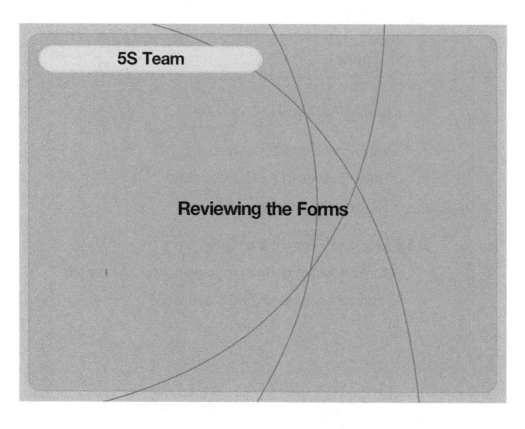

5S Team

Reviewing the Forms

Notes, Slide 39:

_____

_____

_____

_____

_____

_____

5S Map

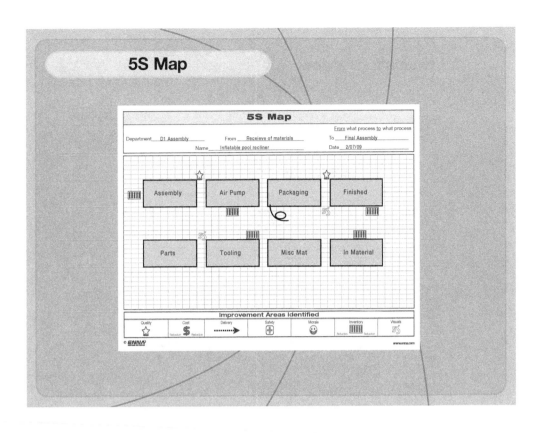

Notes, Slide 40:

_____

_____

_____

_____

_____

_____

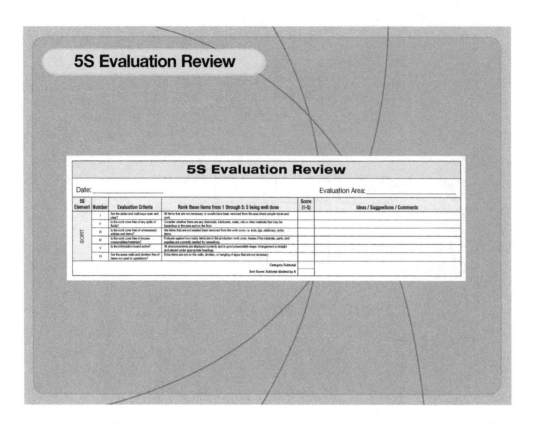

5S Evaluation Review

5S Evaluation Review					

Date: _____   Evaluation Area: _____

5S Element	Number	Evaluation Criteria	Rank these items from 1 through 5; 5 being well done	Score (1-5)	Ideas / Suggestions / Comments
SORT	I	Are the aisles and walkways open and clear?	All items that are not necessary or unsafe have been removed from the area where people travel and work.		
	II	Is the work zone free of any spills of fluids?	Consider whether there are any chemicals, lubricants, water, oils or other materials that may be hazardous in the area and on the floor.		
	III	Is the work zone free of unnecessary articles and items?	Are items that are not needed been removed from the work zone, i.e. tools, jigs, stationary, extra items.		
	IV	Is the work zone free of excess consumables/materials?	Evaluate against how many items are in the production work zone. Assess if the materials, parts, and supplies are currently needed for operations.		
	V	Is the information board active?	All announcements are displayed currently and is good presentable shape. Arrangement is straight and placed under appropriate heading.		
	VI	Are the areas walls and dividers free of items not used in operations?	Extra items are out on the walls, dividers, or hanging of signs that are not necessary.		
			Category Subtotal		
			Sort Score: Subtotal divided by 6		

Notes, Slide 41:

_____

_____

_____

_____

_____

Tip:
Be critical when evaluating the area; the initial evaluation serves as a baseline for further comparison.

Notes, Slide 42:

_____

_____

_____

_____

_____

_____

_____

Tip:

Lighting is key for photographs. Have the team borrow lights to make the items in the pictures really stand out.

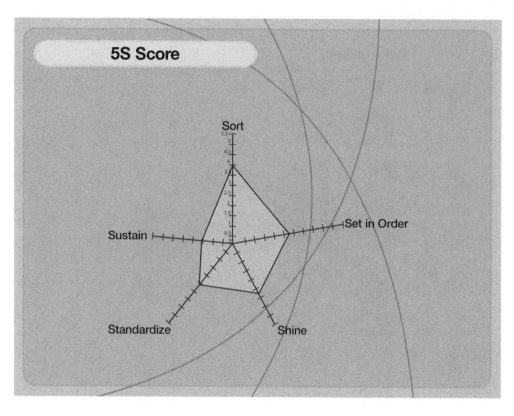

5S Score

Notes, Slide 43:

_____

_____

_____

_____

_____

Tip:
We should be ready to evaluate our current state.

Red Tags/Red Tag Register

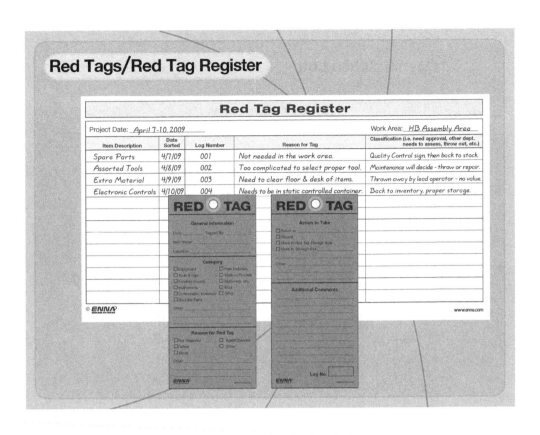

Red Tag Register

Project Date: _April 7-10, 2009_   Work Area: _HB Assembly Area_

Item Description	Date Sorted	Log Number	Reason for Tag	Classification (i.e. need approval, other dept. needs to assess, throw out, etc.)
Spare Parts	4/7/09	001	Not needed in the work area.	Quality Control sign, then back to stock.
Assorted Tools	4/8/09	002	Too complicated to select proper tool.	Maintenance will decide - throw or repair.
Extra Material	4/9/09	003	Need to clear floor & desk of items.	Thrown away by lead operator - no value.
Electronic Controls	4/10/09	004	Needs to be in static controlled container.	Back to inventory, proper storage.

Notes, Slide 44 & 45:

Tip:
If you have any doubt, Red Tag it and "throw it out" of the area.

30 Day 5S Action Log

30 Day 5S Action Log

Start Date: 2/10/2010   Work Area: Reassembly

Date Logged	Item Number	5S Problem	Suggestion to Solve Problem	Who is Responsible
2/15/10	1	Empty Parts Caddy's are	Create a Designated Location/Mark/Label/ID	Jared F.
2/17/10	2	Technicians Steal Clean Up Tools	Create End of Day Clean Up Tool	Henry S.
2/20/10	3	Vendors Cannot Find Their	Visually Designate a Return Parts	Troy G.
2/20/10	4	Towels Used for Soaking Up Water	Fix the Leak Near the Receiving Garge Doors	Jan T.
2/22/10	5	Estimates in Teardown are	Implement Visual Incoming and Outgoing	Jared F.

© ENNA   www.enna.com

Notes, Slide 46:

_____

_____

_____

_____

_____

_____

Tip:

Only place items on the 30 Day 5S Action Log that the team has agreed is an item for that list. Your team should all agree before adding an item to the 30 Day 5S Action Log. You may have to get support from other departments.

5S Sustainment Schedule

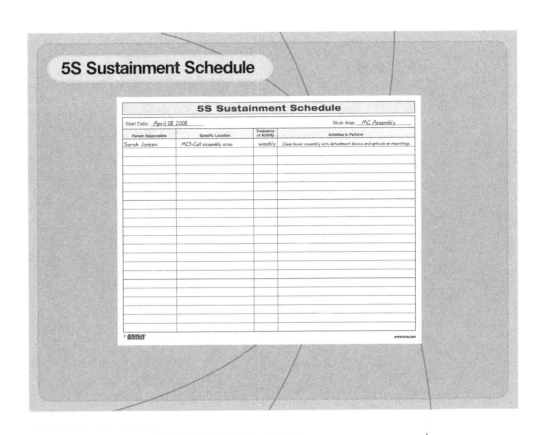

Notes, Slide 47:

_____

_____

_____

_____

_____

_____

_____

Tip:
Team members are expected to commit to 5S by providing innovative ways to solve problems.

5S Board

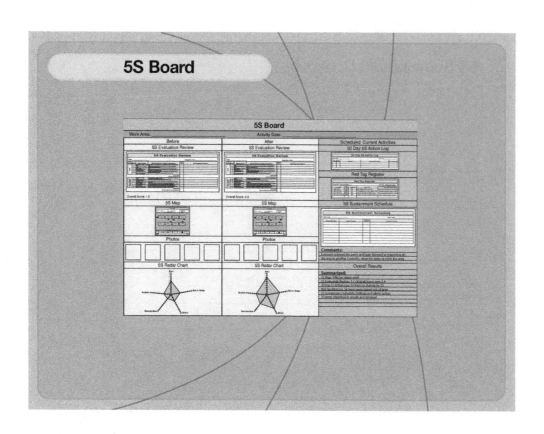

Notes, Slide 48:

_____

_____

_____

_____

_____

_____

5S Assessment

Facilitator: _____   Name: _____

Workshop: _____   Date: _____

Circle or write the answer that best fits the question or completes the statement.

1. _____ 5S originally had _____ S's.
   a) 4
   b) 1
   c) 2

2. _____ What company started what is now known as 5S?
   a) Volvo
   b) Toyota
   c) Ford

3. _____ What is the first S of the 5S's?
   a) Set In Order
   b) Sort
   c) Shine

4. _____ of the 7 Wastes of Operations which one is the worst?
   a) Overproduction
   b) Inventory
   c) Defects

5. _____ If a company implements 5S successfully, the need for self-discipline is _____.
   a) Eliminated
   b) Reduced
   c) Increased

6. _____ 5S is one of the building blocks of _____?
   a) Operations
   b) Cleanliness
   c) Lean

7. _____ Why do we clean during 5S?
   a) To inspect
   b) Because it is the right thing to do
   c) To prevent bad parts

8. _____ What does inventory exist in the company as?
   a) Raw, WIP, FG
   b) GF, WIP, RAW
   c) PIW, WAR, FG

9. _____ The S in Set In Order allows for a person to have minimal _____.
   a) Work
   b) Waiting
   c) Motion

10. _____ What is the 5S Sustainment Schedule used for?
    a) Recording workshop activity
    b) Recording the cleaning that is needed
    c) Scheduling the next workshop

11. _____ For 5S to be successful we need the involvement of _____ .
    a) Top management
    b) Entire department
    c) Everyone

12. _____ The 5S Map provides a simple _____ point of view of the work area.
    a) Bird's eye
    b) Planning
    c) Outline

13. _____ Processing is the hardest waste to find because _____ .
    a) There are so many processes
    b) It may initially seem to be a value-added step
    c) It is totally necessary

14. _____ The 30-Day Action Log allows the company to _____.
    a) Document a list of unsolvable problems
    b) List workshop problems to be solved on one document
    c) Demonstrate its commitment to 5S

1:c, 2:b, 3:b, 4:a, 5:b, 6:c, 7:a, 8:a, 9:c, 10:b, 11:c, 12:a, 13:b, 14:b

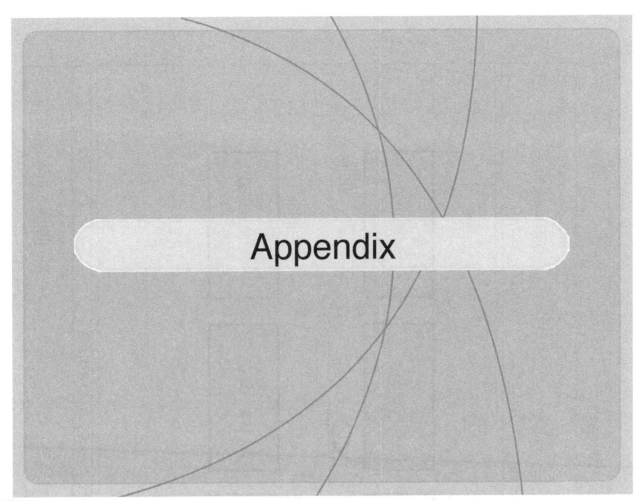

Appendix

Participant Workbook

In this Section

You will find copies of the forms used in the workshop filled out for your reference.

5S Map

Department D1 Assembly

From Receieve of materials

Name Inflatable pool recliner

From what process to what process

To Final Assembly

Date 2/07/09

Assembly

Air Pump

Packaging

Finished

Parts

Tooling

Misc Mat

In Material

Improvement Areas Identified

Quality	Cost	Delivery	Safety	Morale	Inventory	Visuals
	Reduction	Reduction			Reduction	Reduction

© ENNA
KNOWLEDGE INTO PRACTICE

www.enna.com

5S Evaluation Review

Date: _____

Evaluation Area: _____

5S Element	Number	Evaluation Criteria	Rank these items from 1 through 5: 5 being well done	Score (1-5)	Ideas / Suggestions / Comments
SORT	I	Are the aisles and walkways open and clear?	All items that are not necessary or unsafe have been removed from the area where people travel and work.		
	II	Is the work zone free of any spills of fluids?	Consider whether there are any chemicals, lubricants, water, oils or other materials that may be hazardous in the area and on the floor.		
	III	Is the work zone free of unnecessary articles and items?	Are items that are not needed been removed from the work zone, i.e. tools, jigs, stationary, extra items.		
	IV	Is the work zone free of excess consumables/materials?	Evaluate against how many items are in the production work zone. Assess if the materials, parts, and supplies are currently needed for operations.		
	V	Is the information board active?	All announcements are displayed currently and in good presentable shape. Arrangement is straight and placed under appropriate headings.		
	VI	Are the areas walls and dividers free of items not used in operations?	Extra items are not on the walls, dividers, or hanging of signs that are not necessary.		
			Category Subtotal		
			Sort Score: Subtotal divided by 6		

Red Tag Register

Project Date: __April 7-10, 2009__

Work Area: __HB Assembly Area__

Item Description	Date Sorted	Log Number	Reason for Tag	Classification (i.e. need approval, other dept. needs to assess, throw out, etc.)
Spare Parts	4/7/09	001	Not needed in the work area.	Quality Control sign, then back to stock.
Assorted Tools	4/8/09	002	Too complicated to select proper tool.	Maintenance will decide - throw or repair.
Extra Material	4/9/09	003	Need to clear floor & desk of items.	Thrown away by lead operator - no value.
Electronic Controls	4/10/09	004	Needs to be in static controlled container.	Back to inventory, proper storage.

30 Day 5S Action Log

Start Date: 2/10/2010

Work Area: Reassembly

Date Logged	Item Number	5S Problem	Suggestion to Solve Problem	Who is Responsible
2/15/10	1	Empty Parts Caddy's are	Create a Designated Location/Mark/Label/ID	Jared F.
2/17/10	2	Technicians Steal Clean Up Tools	Create End of Day Clean Up Tool	Henry S.
2/20/10	3	Vendors Cannot Find Their	Visually Designate a Return Parts	Troy G.
2/20/10	4	Towels Used for Soaking Up Water	Fix the Leak Near the Receiving Garge Doors	Jan T.
2/22/10	5	Estimates in Teardown are	Implement Visual Incoming and Outgoing	Jared F.

5S Sustainment Schedule

Start Date: ___April 08, 2008___　　　　Work Area: ___MC Assembly___

Person Responsible	Specific Location	Frequency of Activity	Activities to Perform
Sarah Janzen	MC3-Cell assembly area	weekly	Clean lower assembly arm, detachment device, and opticals on mountings.

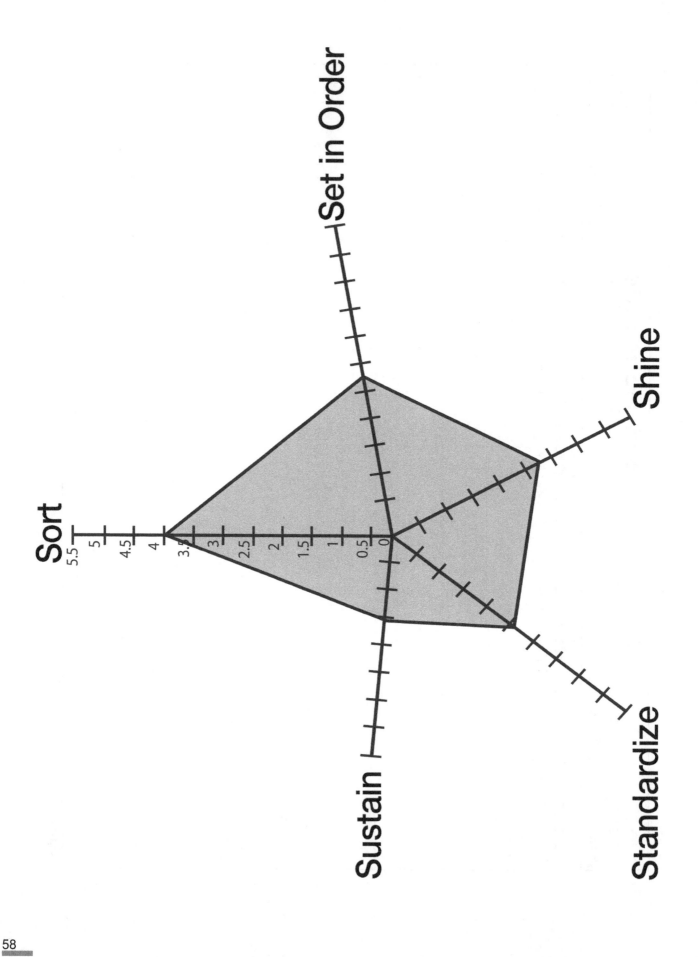